Girls' Club Experience

Louisburg Library
Bringing People and Information Together

As a courtesy to all patrons
Please Do Not Write In Book

You may copy the workbook pages
To practice on

Louisburg Library
Bringing People and Information Together

Girls' Club

EXPERIENCE

A Guided Journey into Friendship

Sally & Joy Clarkson

TYNDALE
MOMENTUM®

*The nonfiction imprint of
Tyndale House Publishers, Inc.*

Visit Tyndale online at www.tyndale.com.

Visit Tyndale Momentum online at www.tyndalemomentum.com.

TYNDALE, *Tyndale Momentum*, and Tyndale's quill logo are registered trademarks of Tyndale House Publishers, Inc. The Tyndale Momentum logo is a trademark of Tyndale House Publishers, Inc. Tyndale Momentum is the nonfiction imprint of Tyndale House Publishers, Inc., Carol Stream, Illinois.

Girls' Club Experience: A Guided Journey into Friendship

Designed by Eva M. Winters

Edited by Stephanie Rische

For information about special discounts for bulk purchases, please contact Tyndale House Publishers at csresponse@tyndale.com, or call 1-800-323-9400.

ISBN 978-1-4964-3611-5

Printed in the United States of America

25   24   23   22   21   20   19
7   6   5   4   3   2   1

❧ Contents ❧

Introduction

Friendship is one of the sweetest gifts in life. It was this deep conviction, based on our happy experience, that drove us to write *Girls' Club*, our collaborative memoir about friendship. We believe friendship has not always been portrayed in the best light in our world, and for that reason, we've sometimes missed its power and beauty. Our hope was to paint a picture of friendship that shows its potential for bringing joy; stirring up growth; and calling us to our best, wisest, strongest selves. But we also feel that painting a picture is not enough. It is our hope that Girls' Club chapters will pop up all over the world.

Friendship must be cultivated, like a garden. A beautiful garden will not grow if you do nothing to tend to the soil, sow seeds, water it regularly, and keep weeds out. Friendships likewise require time, care, questions, intentionality, patience, and love. If *Girls' Club* sparked your imagination for the kind of friendship garden you could grow, perhaps this guidebook will give you the tools and seeds you need to start planting!

This guidebook can be used in several different ways. You may want to start from the beginning and work your way through all the exercises with one friend or a new friend or several different friends. Or you can dip in here and there and work through the chapters that strike you as most interesting or relevant for this stage of your life. Our main hope is that in pondering these questions and activities, you will develop deeper friendships—or even start some new ones. We also hope this book will help you get to know yourself better so you can move into growing intimacy and trust with friends. No matter how you use the book, we think it will be a lot of fun. Spending time with someone who loves you enough to get to know you better not only bonds you with that person but also gives you a bigger vision of who you are.

This book contains practical exercises to help you grow deeper in your friendship as you work through them with a friend or a small group of friends. The goal of each chapter is to draw you out and into a deeper knowledge of and trust in one another. As such, there are a few important ground rules before getting started.

First, be a trustworthy friend, because trust is the foundation of any relationship. This book is meant to invite you into a deep, personal, probing journey. As we share about ourselves with worthy people, our trust in them grows, and we feel more closely connected. But to be able to trust, we must first have a sense of safety. For this reason, before you dive into this guide, we suggest that you make a commitment with your friends about when and how often you will meet. No one wants to feel like they went to a meeting, shared deep parts of themselves, and then never had an opportunity to connect with those people again. Making a commitment to get together for, say, four meetings will create a safe space for you to share and will cultivate a sense of continuity.

Furthermore, you and your friend or group should create some ground rules for discussion. Approach the conversations that spring from this book with humility and kindness. Do not ambush. Do not teach. Do not express harsh criticism, judgment, or contempt. Don't share your friend's secrets or information with anyone else unless you have her permission. Listen actively; do not be distracted; try to care more about what other people say than what you say. You might consider making a no-phones policy for the time you spend together. Promise not to share each other's secrets. Be each other's advocates.

One final note: enjoy the journey! Friendship is a great delight; take it seriously, but seriously enjoy it. In our opinion, food bonds people together like nothing else, so try to eat something delicious together. Laugh and enjoy the process, and if you can, go someplace beautiful or fun. Make this a memorable journey together.

We hope this book will be the catalyst for many deep conversations, belly-aching sessions of laughter, and maybe even a few unexpected friendships.

Peace and love,
Sally and Joy

PART 1

Heart

1

A Friend Knows
Your Story

*My mouth will tell of your righteous acts, of your
deeds of salvation all the day, for their number
is past my knowledge. With the mighty deeds
of the Lord GOD I will come; I will remind
them of your righteousness, yours alone. O God,
from my youth you have taught me, and I still
proclaim your wondrous deeds. So even to old age
and gray hairs, O God, do not forsake me, until
I proclaim your might to another generation,
your power to all those to come.*

PSALM 71:15-18, ESV

*I'm the cover of a book
Whose pages are still being written.*

FROM "BEING A FATHER"
BY RICHARD L. RATLIFF

JOY ✆ Your life is a story.

Sometimes in relationships we find that we know a great deal about someone and yet still feel that we do not really know them. There is some invisible barrier, some untapped knowledge that keeps us at arm's length. I call it the "Facebook problem." You can learn a lot of facts about someone from their posts on social media: their name, their date of birth, where they live and work, their travels. You might even pick up some deeper details: their favorite books, movies, and music. But this knowledge is abstract and disconnected.

To really know someone, you have to know their story.

We speak about our lives as if they are stories. When someone asks how our day has been, we might say something like, "It was good. I woke up this morning, dragged myself out of bed, and was almost late to my 8 a.m. class . . ." or "I took the kids to school, worked at the coffee shop, did laundry . . ." Then we'd go on telling the narrative of our day. We don't rattle off facts; we spin tales.

Instinctively, we all think of our lives as stories. There are beginnings, important introductions, and main characters. There are shining moments of joy and gut-wrenching moments of defeat. We trace our lives looking for the moments of tension, the climax, and the resolution. Our stories are what make sense of the facts about us; they weave together who we are, what we love, what we struggle with, and what we hope for. Who are we apart from our stories?

Our stories are also where we can most clearly see God's hand graciously guiding our lives. Through grateful retrospection, we can see the story lines where He has been faithful and the arcs of promise that are still waiting to be fulfilled.

The bridge from social media knowledge to personal knowledge is story. If we want to be close to someone—to know them and to celebrate who they are—we must know their story. But to know their story, and for ours to be known, we must learn to tell our story and to listen to the stories of others. If we want to move from the distant knowledge of social media friendship to the closeness and intimacy of true friendship, we need to share our life narratives. But we must also return the favor; we must listen to and honor the stories of our friends as well.

All too often, we neglect to tell our stories. One reason we might do so is because this kind of sharing requires time and intentionality—two highly priced commodities in our hurried times. And because our stories comprise so much of who we are, it can feel vulnerable and even embarrassing to share what is closest to our hearts. That's not to say you ought to share your life with everyone; you should only do so with those you trust, those who will honor it appropriately. But if you never tell your story, you will never be known. So be brave, and share with someone. You may even surprise yourself as you discover what an important story it is as you tell it.

Take my word for it: I've never encountered a boring life story yet.

Activities

For this activity, we will learn to thoughtfully share our stories. Perhaps you've never thought of your life as a story before; if that's the case, you are in for an exciting surprise. Before you and your friend or your group get together, take some time to work through the following questions so you can be prepared to tell your story.

You might want to bring some things that are significant to what you are sharing, such as a picture or a keepsake.

1. Create a simple timeline of your life up to this point. What have been the significant events? Moves? Marriage? Divorce? Deaths? Times of special growth? Think about the things that are important to you now (your career, your beliefs, significant people). When did those important things or people enter your life? It might help you to draw a literal line and plot the major events along it.

2. Who are the main characters in your story? What people have shaped who you are, for better or worse? Who loved/loves you? Whom do you love? Who has hurt you? How do those people shape who you are today?

3. What was God doing during the various seasons of your life? Take some time to think and pray about how God has worked and moved. Was there a moment when you first knew God's love for you? What was that like? What prayers have been answered? What prayers have you not seen answered yet?

4. Now that you've taken the time to think through your story, try to consolidate it into a ten-minute (or so) narrative to tell your friends. You can write it out if you want, or you can just bullet-point the significant moments. If you're having a hard time writing this down, remember that your life is a story. Try telling it like this: "Once upon a time, I was born in . . ." or "On a muggy night in Texas, on May 26, I was born . . ." I have no doubt your story is important and interesting.

    I would recommend some ground rules for telling your story. Sharing is vulnerable, because it allows people a peek into who you really are. As such, you and your friend or group of friends should be careful to receive each other's stories attentively and graciously. Honor the life stories of your friends as God honors them; they are infinitely important. As you listen, pay attention to what seems significant, beautiful, and central to who they are. After each person finishes telling her story, allow a few minutes to talk about it. Tell your friend what you think is special about what she shared. Affirm the importance and significance of her journey.

5. Read Hebrews 11 aloud together. This passage, one of the most famous in the New Testament, is simply a collection of the stories of God's faithful people. In their own ways, these stories are testimonies to God's faithfulness and the individual's faith. How might it affect the way you live when you think of your story being among theirs?

Digging Deeper

Read the monologue "All the World's a Stage" (from act II, scene 7 of *As You Like It* by William Shakespeare), which explores the different roles we play over the course of the story of our lives.

A Friend Learns
What You Treasure

*Wherever your treasure is, there the
desires of your heart will also be.*

MATTHEW 6:21

*The gifts we treasure most over the years are often
small and simple. In easy times and in tough times,
what seems to matter most is the way we show those
nearest us that we've been listening to their needs,
to their joys, and to their challenges.*

FRED ROGERS

SALLY ℘ It is possible to have many friends and hundreds of acquaintances and still feel lonely. As a writer of many books, a mother of four adult children who are my best friends, one who has traveled and lived internationally, and someone who has had a lifelong commitment to ministry, I have often felt lonely, even when surrounded by committed people. I long for a kindred spirit— someone who gets me at a heart level, someone who cares about the things that are of great importance to me, someone who will ask me questions and show interest in the things most dear to me.

That last item brings up an important point. Because most of us have to be drawn out and will not share what is on our hearts or what makes us tick unless someone shows personal interest, we might say a friend is one who has learned the art of asking good questions.

How right Jesus was when He said, "Wherever your treasure is, there the desires of your heart will also be." The things on my heart and the thoughts that engage me most frequently are about my husband, my children, my home, my friends, my ministry, what I am writing, and my next adventure. But rare is the person who takes the time to explore these precious treasures of mine. Usually someone wants to tell me about themselves and all that is going on in their own life. Of course, friendships should be reciprocal, and I want to listen to other people's hearts with devoted attention. But I have often left a place wishing someone had asked me a personal question about what mattered to me. I also want people to see inside and affirm me in personal ways.

I love this week's exercise. How fun it is to talk about the things we value most! As you take time to reflect and discuss with your friends this week, have fun and talk about the things you love, even if they are not present in your life at the moment. For instance, if you love to travel and want to take trips, mention this even if you have a job that keeps you homebound or you don't have enough money to travel right now.

Activities

1. A joyful heart is good medicine. Take time this week to remember and catalog all the things you value and enjoy. When we place joyful activities along the paths of our lives, it will indeed be like medicine to our bones, our whole bodies. These things we value and enjoy can be mundane or complex. Ask your friends how you might include more of your preferences in your life. The following is a fun list, but it will also give you a glimpse into some of your friends' preferences (and your own):

   - favorite color
   - favorite clothing style
   - favorite home decor
   - favorite food
   - favorite way to spend an evening
   - favorite thing to save for
   - favorite way to relax
   - favorite thing to do with people
   - favorite place to live (in theory)
   - favorite place to travel (or where you wish you could travel)

2. Review Matthew 6:21 once again.

   - Who or what do you treasure most of all? Or, to ask the question another way, Who or what would you most hate to lose?

- What have you accomplished that you value most? What other goals do you hope to achieve?

- What occupies your dreams and hopes about your future? Where do you want to live or travel to? Who would you love to live near?

- What activities are you passionate about (e.g., exercise, reading, travel, cooking, writing, etc.)? How do you pursue that passion, and what fulfills you most about this area of interest? Tell about a specific time you did this and what was fulfilling about it. For instance, "I loved the years when I could make a big pot of tea, light the candles in my room, and just read for hours. I felt so cozy and inspired, and it refueled my imagination" or "I remember when I ran my first half marathon and was able to keep up with my more experienced friends.

I loved the feeling of accomplishment and strength and health I felt from finishing."

- Describe why you are passionate about each of these interests and how they bring you enjoyment.

3. Ephesians 2:10 says, "We are God's masterpiece. He has created us anew in Christ Jesus, so we can do the good things he planned for us long ago." In the movie *Chariots of Fire*, the main character, Eric Liddell, says, "When I run, I feel His pleasure." When we are living by the drives God gave us, according to our unique personalities and stories, we will feel energized and centered.

- When in your life do you most often feel God's pleasure? What do you feel you were made to do? Or put another way, considering your skill set and drive, what do you think God uniquely created you to do? Maybe this list of words will help: teach, give, help, inspire, encourage, provide, create, write, sing, organize, lead, bring recreation and fun, build, sow, develop others.

- What action or activity makes you feel fulfilled? Give an example of a time this was true.

4. "Whatever you do, do it all for the glory of God" (1 Corinthians 10:31). What is your vision for your life? What would make you feel that you have accomplished what you were created to do? What ideals fill your mind (for example, raising godly kids, teaching college students, writing worship music, helping the poor, becoming a speech and debate judge, helping people heal through counseling, teaching children, nursing those who are

ill, planting gardens, decorating and bringing beauty to home environments, cooking healthy foods)? Take time to share with your friends the dreams you treasure. Each person can share one dream at a time, or each person can have ten minutes to share all at once. Then discuss questions that help open each person's heart in these areas. Here are some possible questions:

- Why is this area of interest important to you?

- When have you felt a great sense of accomplishment?

- What thoughts occupy your mind most often? Where do you get your ideas or inspiration from? How and when do you prepare for this activity?

- Do you ever feel different from others because of this dream you cherish? How can we support you in this?

Digging Deeper

Journal your feelings and thoughts regarding what you learned about yourself and the things you treasure. Be sure to put those dreams and ideals into a plan that can be worked on and exercised in the real-time pathway of your life.

Determine to meet with your friend or friends on a semiregular basis to evaluate the progress you are making in meeting your goals (for example, every birthday lunch or every January 5 or a time that is meaningful for you and your friends).

3

A Friend Hopes
with You

Love never gives up, never loses faith, is always
hopeful, and endures through every circumstance.

I CORINTHIANS 13:7

We must accept finite disappointment,
but never lose infinite hope.

MARTIN LUTHER KING JR.

SALLY ❧ I remember watching the Olympics as a little girl, gathered around our television with my brothers and their friends every night for a couple of weeks. One of our favorite competitions, in my memory, was the steeplechase. This is a race where the competitors have to run a long course that includes jumping over four hurdles and eventually leaping across a menacing water pit. Just when the runner vaulted over one barrier, another was at hand, and then that water pit threatened their demise. Even some of the most talented of the lot fell flat, losing the race in the end. Yet there always seemed to be that strong, focused athlete who had learned, through training, to endure the challenge of the race, to focus on the run with the end in mind. The champion is the one who not only runs and jumps well but cherishes the belief that they can finish the task.

From my perspective as a woman in my midsixties, I perceive that life is a steeplechase with endless hurdles and water pits to overcome along the way. Over the course of a lifetime, most of us will encounter financial challenges, difficult relationships, daunting questions, personal disappointments, health issues, faith crises, and more. On the pathway of life, we will also cherish dreams of what we might accomplish, ideals we hold dear, and meaningful commitments we hope to make.

When we have strong friends to walk beside us, we are much more likely to stay faithful to our ideals, to pursue the dreams of our hearts, to be faithful in our relationships within marriage and with family and friends, and to be strong in life. When we have hope, we are more likely to mount up over obstacles and to endure life's hurdles with grace.

In my investigations about hope, here is one definition I came across: "Hope is an optimistic state of mind that is based on an expectation of positive outcomes with respect to events and circumstances in one's life or the world at large. When we find life challenging our confidence or belief that we can finish or accomplish a goal or have the strength to pursue an ideal, hope is the invisible attribute of the heart that will carry us through to the end."

We often keep the things we hope for closely guarded because we have difficulty sharing some of our hopes and dreams. But it's important to share our hopes, because the affirmation of others in those moments fuels our hearts. It plants in us the will to keep pursuing an ideal or a commitment.

Remember, a friend is not called to question or challenge one's hope but to listen and understand and support. While it's true that giving wisdom when another asks is a part of being a friend, in this exercise today you are encouraged to listen to the hopes of your friend with an uncritical eye, with the idea of understanding her heart better.

How we support our friends in their search for hope and confidence varies from one person to the next according to their unique needs. Some people need loving words; others may need physical support or financial help or training. Each of us receives encouragement in a different way. As you go through this activity, focus on listening to the other person's heart and seek to show sympathy in the way they feel most supported.

An added advantage is that by taking the time to search your own heart, you will discover things bubbling up inside that you may not have even been aware were there. Give yourself at least an hour to answer these questions for yourself. Then share a cup of tea or coffee in a private place—a café or a corner of your home—so you can have uninterrupted time and privacy to share what is in your hearts.

Be specific and honest. Everything you hope for, no matter how remote or unusual, is important. When your friend understands the hopes you store in your heart, she will better know how to support you.

Activities

1. "If you need wisdom, ask our generous God, and he will give it to you. He will not rebuke you for asking" (James 1:5). Are there any ways in which your dreams or hopes are in conflict with God's principles of wisdom for your life? Take some time to pray about your hopes, asking God to reveal to you if there are any dreams that aren't of Him or if there are things He desires for you that you haven't opened yourself to yet.

2. "Faith shows the reality of what we hope for; it is the evidence of things we cannot see" (Hebrews 11:1). Often, God calls us to believe in what we cannot see. Hope is the fuel that keeps us moving forward as we pursue what we think God is calling us to. The challenges that cause us to lose hope might be

feelings of weariness or external obstacles. A part of working through these challenges is learning to see what is in your heart so you can invite a friend to walk this road with you.

Take at least an hour to write down the things you hope for in your life. (Consider areas such as strengthening your marriage, raising your children, furthering your education, healing a broken relationship, getting a certain job, seeing doors open for a dream you would like to accomplish, moving to a certain location, being healed of an illness, going on a trip, or anything else you wish would come to fruition in your life.) God sees us for who we are, and He longs for us to trust Him with all that is in our hearts. Try to put a searchlight on some of the issues you have been holding and might now be aware of. Be specific and give details. Here are some examples to get you started:

- I would like to move to a place with land, at least five acres, in a town near my parents [or near the ocean or mountains].
- I regret having fought with my parents (or a friend), and I want to reconcile with them.
- I have failed in something important to me, and I wish I could get over my feelings of insecurity.
- I would like to start a ministry to women or children who have experienced divorce in their families (or to refugees or troubled youth) to help them heal and find a way forward in their lives.
- I would like to write a book and become an author.
- I wish I could travel to a certain country or learn another language.
- I would like to get out of debt and save enough money to move my family into an apartment.
- I would like to pursue my degree at a particular college.
- I wish I could get my husband to go to counseling with me so that we can be closer.

3. "Anyone who wants to come to him must believe that God exists and that he rewards those who sincerely seek him" (Hebrews 11:6). There are so many challenges to hope, both internal and external. That's why hope requires such courage on our part. It's helpful to think through some of those potential obstacles so we are prepared when they come our way.

- What fears swim through your heart that make you feel these hopes are impossible?

- What has kept you from moving towards your dreams?

- What thoughts discourage you from enduring difficult situations with faith?

- Think of a specific challenge you're facing right now. What do you think God might be calling you to believe about this situation?

4. "So you see, faith by itself isn't enough. Unless it produces good deeds, it is dead and useless" (James 2:17). Name three practical ways you can cultivate hope or faith in the midst of a difficult situation you are facing. Find ways you might move in the direction of your hopes, and list practical ideas of how to move forward.

5. Give each person about twenty minutes to share her hopes. Spend ten minutes each responding to one another's hopes. Close your time praying together about how God might work in these areas. Remember that your friends' hopes are very precious to them. Listen to them with full focus—the same way you would want them to listen to you. Listening with your heart and mind is a skill that will pave the way for others to trust you. Learn to give sympathetic responses to those sharing with you, such as the following:

"I am so grateful you were willing to share that with me."
"How can I help you feel understood and supported right now?"
"What makes you feel understood and encouraged? Words of affirmation? Physical help? Time together to work on this project? Praying together?"

Remember that there are no specific rules as you share these answers, but focus on understanding and helping the other person feel heard. As you do so, you will find your friendship getting closer, one hope at a time. Take some time to pray together about what has been shared, with each person praying for another friend.

PART 2
❧ Soul ❧

4

A Friend Helps You Discover
Your Core Values

Don't let your special character and values,
the secret that you know and no one else does,
the truth—don't let that get swallowed up
by the great chewing complacency.

AESOP

Do not waver, for a person with divided loyalty
is as unsettled as a wave of the sea that is
blown and tossed by the wind.

JAMES 1:6

JOY ✐ I remember vividly the panic of graduating from college.

After all the exams, handshakes, high heels, and pictures, the reality of life after college was beginning to set in. Until graduation, there had always been an obvious next step, but suddenly the world was laid ahead of me with a thousand thrilling and terrifying possibilities. The weight of my decisions settled heavy on me. My next step felt significant and scary. Should I choose a job close to home? Or the perfect graduate program far, far away? How was I to know what to choose?

When I arrived back home in Colorado, my mother quickly noticed the permanent and increasing arch of my worried eyebrows. Like any good friend would, she took me to brunch to sort it out. After we finished eating, with coffee in hand, my mom pulled out a list of questions. They were about everything from my lifestyle preferences (city, suburbia, country) to my relational needs (community, friends, church) to my deepest sense of passion and calling. As we talked, the choices I needed to make and the life I wanted to live began to take shape. My love of research and writing, and my desire to teach and mentor, cut away some career options. My need and love for like-minded friends and community led me to look for a place to live where I could find such people. My thirst for adventure, my desire to meet people outside the box of my world and to let my soul be shaped by more than the suburb in Southern California where I had attended college caused me to look for places that would (affordably) open those doors.

As the options for what I would do next began to crystallize, it became clear that my mom was not just helping me unearth my preferences or ideal living/working situation; she was helping me unearth my core values as a person—what I loved, cherished, thrived on, and was called to.

Our values guide our decisions in life. Even if we aren't conscious of it, our choices say something about our values. To choose one thing and not another is to elevate one value over another. Our values function as a sort of compass, pulling us towards a particular way of life. Therefore, if we want to live life well, we need to be conscious of what our values are and how they affect the way we live.

Our values will play out in different ways depending on our unique personalities and experiences. But as we grow in Christ and in maturity, our values ought to be shaped by our walk with God and become clear, strong, guiding principles for our decisions. A good friend, like my mom, will help us discover and articulate our values. I've often found that friends are able to see things about me that I cannot, and they are able to help me see what I value.

Once we know what our values are, friends help us live faithfully according to them. When we start to stray off the path, friends lovingly call us back to the commitments, loves, and values we cherish. When we are struggling, our friends help us unearth and name our values. When we forget what is most important, our friends remind us. When we live fruitfully according to what is important, our friends celebrate and cheer us on.

That day over brunch, my mom helped me sort through the confusion of obligations and pressures to discover my core values. With a clear vision of what I valued, my decisions felt less like burdens and more like opportunities to shape my life around what I loved, what I felt called to, and who I was. Friends help us discover those values and live vibrantly and faithfully into them.

Activities

1. Look through the following list of words and circle your top five values. Don't circle what you think you ought to value; circle the words that jump off the page at you, the ones that capture your imagination. And if you think of something that's not on there, feel free to add it.

   - honesty
   - humor
   - family
   - achievement
   - hospitality
   - integrity
   - wisdom
   - education
   - adventure
   - authenticity
   - compassion
   - fairness
   - friendship
   - fun
   - simplicity
   - loyalty
   - hard work
   - openness
   - piety
   - kindness
   - justice
   - creativity
   - competence
   - independence
   - harmony

2. With your friends, discuss the values you circled, working through the following questions:

- Why are these values particularly important to you?

- When in your life have these values taken priority?

- How do you see these values working themselves out in your life?

- Did any of your friends' values surprise or interest you? Why?

3. Not every value is inherently good. We should carefully think through what we value and whether it is lifegiving and God honoring. Matthew 6:24 says, "No one can serve two masters. For you will hate one and love the other; you will be devoted to one and despise the other." It is possible for our values to come into conflict with our faith, the good of others, or even our own good. Is there anything you are valuing that might threaten the health of your relationship with God or others, or keep you from living fully into God's call on your life?

4. Take time to encourage one another in living according to your core values. Share about the following topics:

  • Which of these values do you feel like you're living out most faithfully?

  • Which of these values is falling by the wayside?

  • What is keeping you from living according to your values?

5. Think of one thing you can do this week to live more in line with one of your values. The next time you get together, check in to see how that pursuit is going.

Digging Deeper

Jane Eyre is the story of someone who is so assured of her values (honesty, integrity, freedom) that she makes good and difficult life decisions to stay faithful to those values. Watch one of the movie adaptations with a friend and discuss it.

5

A Friend Cheers On Your Passions

I would rather die of passion than of boredom.

ÉMILE ZOLA

*Never be lacking in zeal, but
keep your spiritual fervor, serving the Lord.*

ROMANS 12:11, NIV

SALLY ✋ Fifth grade brought unexpected trials to my little-girl life. Our family had moved to Houston, and I ended up spending two and a half of the four months we lived there in the hospital or in bed. I had a chronic case of double pneumonia that just would not go away. Having been a premature baby, born at six and a half months and weighing just three pounds, I had battled respiratory infections and asthma my whole life. Eventually we discovered that I was highly allergic to mildew and mold. Consequently, we moved again, this time to New Mexico, where the climate was dry and without mold, and where I could breathe.

As I look back, I actually remember the months in bed as a time of awakening. My mother, seeking to help me pass the lonely hours with some entertainment, asked my teacher if she could recommend some books that would captivate my attention. I read literally hundreds of pages that awakened dreams in my heart I had never known before. Biographies became favorites as I read about person after person who had changed their world. Wilma Rudolph, the champion runner who won against all odds. Florence Nightingale, who saved hundreds of lives by assisting wounded soldiers and transforming medical-practice routines. And then there was *A Wrinkle in Time*, which captured my imagination as it described a young girl who fought against darkness by exercising the power of love.

It was during this season of reading that I began to understand that I was a dreamer, one who would imagine myself a hero in my own story and conjure up ways I could influence the world. I longed to do something significant with my life, and I had confidence growing in my heart that would eventually help open those doors.

Yet when these thoughts and feelings persisted into adulthood and I shared my ideas with others, they would often give me some logical reason why my dreams would never become reality.

Me: I want to become a writer who inspires people.

Response: Thousands of people dream of publishing a book, but only a very small fraction actually ever secure a contract. You probably just need to get a regular job.

Me: I want to go into missions in Communist countries and help others know Jesus better.

Response: Aren't you embarrassed to have to ask people for money? And I have heard it is not safe for women to work behind the Iron Curtain. Why don't you just stay home like normal people? There's a lot of good mission work to do right here at home.

Over the years I began to learn that if I was going to dream of how God might use me, very few people would agree with my dreams of a different sort of life, and I would probably be somewhat lonely.

Then when I was in college, along came a friend and mentor who had something different to say to me: "Sal, I think you are a gifted message maker. I think God is going to use you to encourage many people in your lifetime."

She made me believe that maybe God did have something significant for me to do, and I kept her words alive in the secret places of my heart. Later I met another friend who came alongside me and said, "Let's both go to Poland and use our apartment to be a place where people feel the love of Jesus through our meals and Bible studies. Let's do it together." My heart breathed in the welcome from someone who believed in the dreams I cherished, someone who understood me and shared the passions of my heart. My inner dreams and my outer commitments were finally aligned.

I have never quit dreaming or taking risks or following the ideals God has placed on my heart. A handful of people truly get me, and they have kept me going forward. These friends who talk the same language of life as I do are the ones who have become my inner circle. As my daughters, Sarah and Joy, grew up, that circle expanded to include them. As I shared my ideals with them, they took on my passions for themselves, and now we dream together as kindred spirits.

It is a rare woman who takes the time to look beyond her own personality and story to embrace and champion the inspirations of her friend. In this activity, you will have the opportunity to place a searchlight in your heart and soul to find the passions bubbling up there. Then you can ask yourself, *How might the Holy Spirit work through me in my lifetime to bring His light to bear through my personal story?*

If we believe that God has crafted our unique personalities and passions for His purposes, we will understand that we were made by the Creator for good works—works He planned for us even before we took our first breath (Ephesians 2:10).

Activities

1. Take an online personality test with your friend. Answer according to who you are at the deepest and most authentic level. (My favorite tests are usually the ones associated with the

Myers-Briggs Type Indicator. This tool has helped everyone in our family find their footing within the design of their own personalities. It has allowed us to learn and understand how we might thrive in life and what would be a burden to our particular type.)

Discuss the results with a friend or your family. When it comes to personality issues, all preferences are neutral. In other words, someone who prefers helping others or teaching others is no better or worse than someone who wants to build houses or design landscapes. All of us are created within the boundaries of our personalities to do something for the glory of God. And our passions will differ according to our call in life.

2. List eight words that define you (for instance: bold, visionary, creative, stable, strong, compassionate, flexible, practical, quiet, lover, truth teller, organizer, beautifier, encourager, debater, etc.). Then write a short sentence about how you have seen these attributes work out in your life.

3. In no more than two paragraphs, complete this statement:
   "If money were no object and there were no other limitations,
   I would love to accomplish _____ in my
   lifetime."

4. Write a paragraph about what you would like to be remembered
   for. For what purpose do you think you have been made?

5. Write down some areas of interest that you love to share with
   others. For instance, here are some of mine:

   - *Motherhood:* mentoring my children to fulfill their emotional,
     spiritual, mental, and physical potential
   - *Discipleship:* passing on the love of Christ and motivating others
     to follow Him their whole lives
   - *Teaching the Bible:* making the truths of Scripture come alive
     for both mature believers and new followers of Christ

Other areas of interest might include opening a natural foods café, becoming a nurse in a cancer ward for children, building a home for single moms and their children, buying a big house with land where people can come for training, becoming an international journalist, gardening and harvesting your own vegetables for your meals, becoming a singer-songwriter, developing an online website to encourage people with mental illness, getting married and having lots of kids, buying a house for your family, etc.

6. Circle which of the following areas are passions that drive you to work for your ideals:

- healthy eating
- music
- art
- education
- gardening
- creating beautiful environments
- cooking
- building
- teaching
- traveling
- hosting

- performing
- speaking
- writing
- working with computers
- designing cities, neighborhoods, hospitals, schools, etc.
- politics
- international diplomacy
- painting or drawing
- philosophy
- theology

With your friend, take fifteen minutes each to describe some of the passions and dreams that are on your heart. If you had no limitations, what would you like to do in this season of your life? Respond to your friend by showing empathy and support for her dreams and aspirations. Ask how you can encourage her in those areas.

6

A Friend Encourages You to Cultivate Your Gifts

In his grace, God has given us different gifts for doing certain things well. So if God has given you the ability to prophesy, speak out with as much faith as God has given you. If your gift is serving others, serve them well. If you are a teacher, teach well. If your gift is to encourage others, be encouraging. If it is giving, give generously. If God has given you leadership ability, take the responsibility seriously. And if you have a gift for showing kindness to others, do it gladly.

ROMANS 12:6-8

The place God calls you to is the place where your deep gladness and the world's deep hunger meet.

FREDERICK BUECHNER

JOY ✑ I remember watching a documentary once about coral reefs. The rich-voiced narrator described the great collection of living creatures that make up these vibrant underwater worlds, and how fish of every shape, size, and brilliant color swim, slither, and dance through the chasms. There are corals that are soft and squelchy; chalky, hard growth that covers the face of rocks; and grass-like plants that wave and hide playful fish. The narrator described these reefs as delicate ecosystems. The health of the entire reef is dependent upon each strange and unique organism living and thriving and doing its job—the plants purifying the water, the fish doing maintenance of the plants, the corals providing a home for the fish. Without each part doing its job, the reef tumbles quickly towards destruction.

As I watched the documentary, the thought struck me: *This is how it is with us and our God-given gifts.* I believe God created each of us with innate inclinations, gifts, and personalities. When we cultivate them, they can contribute to the health and beauty of our relationships, community, and world. There is no set list of "right," "good," or "perfect" gifts to have; we are as diverse as the many life forms on a coral reef. But without our full-hearted participation in the world, our "ecosystem" will struggle. Do you know how important your life is in God's design? A coral's gift is simply being a coral; your gifts are simply the things you do when you are most yourself. They are the natural outcome of a flourishing you. Your gifts play out in the roles you gravitate towards, your natural proclivities, the things that bring you joy when you do them well.

I am inclined to think that the gifts that come most naturally to us are often the most mysterious; we often don't even notice we are doing them. It is difficult to cultivate gifts we do not know we have. That's where friends can be helpful, acting as mirrors for us and reflecting the things we naturally gravitate towards.

Once we realize what those gifts are, we must take an active part in cultivating them. Good friends encourage us in this endeavor, and they will cheer us on when we use our gifts for the good of others. However, to be able to do this for our friends requires us to lay aside competitiveness and comparison. It is nonsensical for the fish to compete with the coral; each is needed for the health of the reef. We must learn to notice and celebrate the unique skills and gifts of our friends rather than seeing them as a threat to our own competence.

Our gifts are not intended just for us; they come with an obligation. In our highly individualistic world, we do not like to think of obligations; it does violence to our sense of independence. But when we think of the world as a coral reef, we will realize that to withhold our gifts from the world or to not cultivate them is to withhold health from the world. We should never let our friends squander their gifts; we should lovingly encourage them to be good stewards of their place in the reef.

Activities

1. Sometimes other people can see our gifts better than we can. Give everyone in your group a chance to chat about the gifts they've noticed in each person. What role does each person tend to play in your group? What need do they specifically meet? How do they uniquely feed the life of your friendship? What gift do you think is at the root of the role they play? A number of gifts will likely emerge in these conversations. How do they complement one another?

2. Share with the group what you think your gifts are. When do you feel most like yourself, most fulfilled? What do you think you are particularly good at? What role do you often find yourself taking on in your relationships or job?

3. Now that you have an idea of your giftings, discuss how well you are cultivating and using these gifts. Do you feel that you are contributing to the life of the reef with your giftings? What is one way you could use your giftings for the good of others? If your gift is lying dormant right now, how could you move towards using that gift?

4. One of the fruits of a deep friendship—and often the catalyst for one—is the use of your conglomerate giftings for ministry or charity, for the love and life of others. Daydream together about how God could use the combination of your gifts to help others. Perhaps you could organize an event, a club, or meals for a family going through a difficult time, or you could create a magazine full of lifegiving ideas. Pray about whether this is something God is calling you to do together.

PART 3
Mind

7

A Friend Challenges You
to Think Clearly and Biblically

Don't copy the behavior and customs of this world,
but let God transform you into a new person
by changing the way you think. Then you will
learn to know God's will for you, which is good
and pleasing and perfect.

ROMANS 12:2

If you or I were dealing with a mind that was
growing morbid, we should be chiefly concerned
not so much to give it arguments as to give it air,
to convince it that there was something cleaner and
cooler outside the suffocation of a single argument.

G. K. CHESTERTON

JOY ✐ "Talk to your thoughts," my mentor used to say. It's a funny thing to say, really. As a sixteen-year-old, I puzzled over it. Didn't talking to my thoughts merely mean thinking other thoughts? Thinking at my thoughts? What a tangle I got my mind into! However, after years of trying to follow this advice, I've realized how very sound it is. Her point was that we should all recognize that just because we think something doesn't mean it's true. We must be careful to question our own thoughts and beliefs, making sure they are formed by what is true, beautiful, and good.

We can become convinced of ideas about ourselves and our world more out of habit than out of thoughtfulness. Our thinking habits are just like our other habits; they are formed by our experiences, our personalities, the people who speak into our lives, the culture we live in, the information we've been exposed to. Perhaps this is why we can look back on the beliefs of people from the past with incredulity. "How could they believe that?" we ask. But do we think we are immune to such errors ourselves? We are just as formed by our moment in history and our culture as previous generations were. If we do not talk to our thoughts, we will be every bit as susceptible to the whims and half-wisdoms of our day.

I think this is what Paul meant in Romans when he said, "Don't copy the behavior and customs of this world," but instead change the way you think. He is instructing us to resist passive acceptance of whatever the wisdom of our present day is and instead to have a mind renewed and formed by the lasting truths of the gospel. We must align our minds with timeless truth and Scripture-shaped discernment, not with whatever fad of belief or opinion is moving through culture at the moment. This requires a certain level of self-reflection—a willingness to question our own assumptions and to wrestle with the tensions of wisdom. My mentor was right: we must talk to our thoughts.

But the trouble is, we cannot really think our way out of false or sloppy thinking. Our thoughts got us there to begin with. Since it is not always easy to see those blind spots, we must learn to be shaped by Scripture and encourage our friends to do the same.

We ought not to read our Bibles only to discover crystalline truths to apply to every sticky situation we face. While Scripture is certainly full of wisdom, its main purpose is not as a guidebook but rather as a place where we encounter the story of God's dealings and character. As we read, we are formed and shaped by God's story rather than the world's. Reading the Bible not only teaches us the values of the Kingdom but shapes our hearts and minds to love them. We should allow the Bible to form our way of seeing the world.

This is where we need friends who are deeply invested in renewing their own minds and brave enough to gently confront us and draw us back to those habits that will form a wise, loving, and strong mind. A life-giving friendship will not entrench us in self-righteous certainty or the malaise of indifference and skepticism. My dearest friendships are with people who are actively invested in thinking clearly, lovingly, and biblically, and who inspire me to do the same.

Only by talking to our thoughts, instead of blindly accepting them as true, can we begin to be free from the damaging voices of our past, the ever-mumbling cacophony of culture, and the shadow of our own predispositions. Wise friends challenge us to renew our minds and draw us back to Scripture.

Activities

1. Thinking about how we think is half the battle when it comes to renewing our minds; so often our thought life is shaped by things we don't even notice. Take some time to talk through the most significant factors that have influenced how you think about life. Perhaps you will be surprised, but don't feel guilty about any of your answers. In the following categories, who or what has most shaped your thinking?

   – People (parents, siblings, friends, teachers, professors, pastors, mentors, etc.)

   – Books, lectures, movies, or music

   – Social movements, a church, organizations, or religious or political movements

– Your own personality, background, and preferences

– Scripture passages or spiritual practices

– Experiences

As you talked through these areas, did any of your influences come as a surprise? In what ways do you copy the customs of this world rather than being transformed by changing your thinking? (Oh, and by the way, we all have areas where this is the case.) What are the most lifegiving influences on the way you think? Do you sense any blind spots or untruths that you want to reform?

2. Read Proverbs 8–9. Isn't it interesting that wisdom is personified as a woman? I also love the picture of how she invites people to receive wisdom: not just through teaching, but by inviting them into an experience of wisdom where their hearts can be softened and opened and taught. What do you think this communicates about the way we do not just retain wisdom but are shaped by it?

3. Discuss the importance of talking and not yelling about our thoughts. I think one of the reasons we avoid talking with friends about the life of our mind is because we associate it with argument, conflict, and irresolvable differences. But read this passage out loud together:

> Who among you is wise and understanding? Let him show by his good behavior his deeds in the gentleness of wisdom. But if you have bitter jealousy and selfish ambition in your heart, do not be arrogant and so lie against the truth. This wisdom is not that which comes down from above, but is earthly, natural, demonic. For where jealousy and selfish ambition exist, there is disorder and every evil thing. But the wisdom from above is first pure, then peaceable, gentle, reasonable, full of mercy

and good fruits, unwavering, without hypocrisy. And
the seed whose fruit is righteousness is sown in peace by
those who make peace.

JAMES 3:13-18, NASB

I love how this passage notes that true wisdom is not defen-
sive and does not cause divisiveness. This does not mean that
our convictions will never differ from or bump up against those
of our friends. But if we are walking by the Spirit and being
formed by the Word, our thinking will be shaped by a wisdom that is "peaceable, gentle, reasonable [other translations
say "willing to yield"], full of mercy and good fruits." In our
world of angry tweet storms and Facebook arguments, we have
often forgotten this. What would it look like for you to grow
in this kind of wisdom, in relation to both your friends and the
broader world?

8

A Friend Inspires You to Be Curious

*It is God's privilege to conceal things and
the king's privilege to discover them.*

PROVERBS 25:2

*The important thing is not to stop questioning.
Curiosity has its own reason for existence. One
cannot help but be in awe when he contemplates
the mysteries of eternity, of life, of the marvelous
structure of reality. It is enough if one tries merely
to comprehend a little of this mystery each day.*

ALBERT EINSTEIN

JOY ✐ One of my favorite activities is making playlists. Each year I make at least three of them: autumn/winter, Christmas, and spring/summer. This became a cherished tradition several years ago, and now I relish the chance to discover new music, remember old favorites, and prepare for a new season with new tunes. For this reason, I am always on the lookout for new artists, and I always have my finger on the pulse of the music world.

I suppose you could say I am a compulsive music listener. I think I got it from my mother, who carries around her mini speaker playing symphonic sound tracks and gentle piano pieces; we always joke that she comes with her own sound track. In my mind, there are very few situations that could not be bettered by good music: cooking, driving, dinner parties, work, exercise. And I delight in finding just the right artist, sound, and mood for each moment.

"You're my playlist expert," Sarah once said to me. I felt rather pleased with myself. I was happy that my curiosity could bring happiness and light to someone else's life.

Curiosity always begins with a question. The word *question* comes from the same root in Latin as *quest*. Therefore, to ask a question is to begin a quest! When we follow our curiosity about something—music, cooking, history, science, exercise—we set out on a journey to uncover mysteries and meet interesting people along the way.

Each one of us has something about which we are naturally curious, naturally delighted, naturally motivated. These topics can range from the trivial to the profound, and I think both extremes are important. The smaller interests, such as my love of music and songwriters, grow in us a delight in the world. They fill our hearts with hope and make us more interesting people. Even the small curiosities are worth pursuing. But the deep, troubling curiosities of life can be the things that lead us into our callings. Some people, in embarking on the question of why there is suffering, have found themselves giving their life to the alleviation of others' suffering. We all see the world a little differently, through the lens of our personalities and preferences, and each perspective reveals a little more about this multivalent, glistening world and about the character of its Creator.

In friendship we get the delight of peering into the way someone else sees the world, being drawn into their curiosities. As such, we should celebrate the diversity of interests our friends have. And we should inspire each other to become masters of our curiosities—people who are interesting, knowledgeable, delighted, and deep. We should be motivators for each other, keeping alive our wonder and curiosity in this marvelous world that God loves.

Activities

1. Friends are *interesting* and *interested* people. There is no more fun way to get closer to your friends than finding out what piques their interest, what they're passionate about, and what they spend their time thinking about. Talk through the following questions to learn more about the curiosities of your friend:

   * What is one topic you know a lot about? Do you consider yourself a master of any subject/activity/area of interest? What category could you win in a trivia show?

- What do you find yourself thinking about in your spare time for fun (i.e., not for school or work or church)?

- What is something that has always bothered you? What difficult question do you find yourself frequently returning to? How has that question impacted the way you live your life?

- What do your curiosities say about your personality? What have you discovered about the world or about God through your interests?

2. Friends ought to be our greatest encouragers when it comes to cultivating our delights and interests. Encourage each other by asking the questions below.

   - What is one thing you would learn more about if you had the time and money?

- What is one step you could take to learn more about that thing?

- Are there any curiosities you share as friends? Could you learn something together—perhaps through a book club, a cooking class, or a concert?

3. Philippians 4:8 says, "Dear brothers and sisters, one final thing. Fix your thoughts on what is true, and honorable, and right, and pure, and lovely, and admirable. Think about things that are excellent and worthy of praise." Another reason it is important for us to cultivate our interests and passions is because it will fill our hearts with true, honorable things. In our world where there is a constant influx of information, it can be easy to feed our minds on vapid, depressing, or crude things. To resist the soul-numbing effects of this empty stream of information, we must make a battle plan to fill the treasure box of our hearts and minds with true, beautiful, and good treasures from which we can draw. Discuss the following questions to strategize how to fill your treasure box:

- *Truth:* What are you doing to cultivate truth in your heart? What could you do to invest more in this area? What books, podcasts, or publications could you consume to pour more truth into your life?

- *Beauty:* How are you making space for beauty in your life? How could you be more intentional about doing this? What lifegiving book or movie have you been wanting to check out? Could you go on a hike or a picnic to see the beauty of Creation?

- *Goodness:* How are you growing in character? What makes you want to do what is right and good? What is an area of morality, ethics, or character that interests you?

9

A Friend Holds You Accountable

As iron sharpens iron, so
a friend sharpens a friend.

PROVERBS 27:17

I don't need a friend who changes when
I change and who nods when I nod;
my shadow does that much better.

PLUTARCH

SALLY ℘ The air was chill and the sun was barely peeking through the clouds, but an excitement bubbled up from somewhere inside as I thought about the delight of spending time with my friend. As always, she listened to me chatter on about life. We giggled at the same kinds of humor. My struggles and messes and pressures seemed to align with what was on her heart.

There was also the pleasure of how much I enjoyed walking our three-mile route on the mountain path each day. Happy hormones always surged through me as I came around the last curve of the rocky trail. Penny, our faithful golden retriever, ran ahead to drink gulps of water from the pond that marked our finish line. The joy of growing stronger, becoming fitter, and losing weight added to the sense of accomplishment and overall enjoyment of this jaunt with my friend.

Fast-walking five times a week had become a regular commitment for the previous nine months. Now it was such a habit of my life, I was disappointed when something like snow or rain or an out-of-town trip kept us from meeting.

Looking back, I realize that having this commitment and accountability with a friend kept me getting out of bed and being faithful. Somewhere amid the days of repeating this discipline over and over, I stopped thinking of it as a challenge and began to enjoy it as one of the most satisfying times in my week.

I am convinced that this pattern of walking I established with my friend is one of the reasons I am such an avid walker today. All those years ago, it brought such a sense of fulfillment and accomplishment, and I wanted to continue that even after we moved to another part of the country. Part of the reason this routine was so dear to me is that when you invest time with a friend on a regular basis—especially when it involves time to talk and engage in friendship—your heart is bound to be filled and watered with the love and satisfaction of companionship.

Making pacts with friends to commit to a certain goal is a necessary discipline, one that develops excellence in our character that we might not attain otherwise. To be committed to a friend who is excellent in character, loving in relationship, growing in mind and heart, and given to generous serving of others with their time and finances calls me to become the most excellent person I can be in all areas of my life. I have had the privilege of being accountable to precisely these kinds of friends over the years. These experiences have taught me the value of accountability, and it's something I have been committed to ever since. I seek out and meet with women who call me to my best self. As Scripture says, "Walk with the wise and become wise; associate with fools and get in trouble" (Proverbs 13:20).

Accountability is a word that is used frequently, but what does it actually mean? In my view, it means being responsible to someone for a commitment or duty or activity you have undertaken. When we are responsible to another person for our behavior or ideals or work, we feel a great emotional pull to be faithful because we know someone is depending on us to keep our promise. The verse at the beginning of this chapter, which compares friendship to iron sharpening iron, is a picture of accountability. When an iron blade is rubbed against another iron blade, the edges become sharper. The metals rub off the rough edges and make the knife more useful.

When a friendship is an accountable relationship, it calls us to live into our full potential in all areas of our lives.

Over the years I have come to understand how important accountability is for me as a mother. Because I love my children so much and because I want the best for them, I am more diligent to have integrity. I want to be the best model I can be so they can follow my example. I stay more faithful to my ideals because I want them to be able to be faithful to their ideals.

Athletes usually run faster, swim a better race, or play a better football game when they have trained with teammates who push them to do their best. There is a natural power that is released when we know someone is sharpening us or holding a high standard for us. This is the positive power of friendship. In contrast, when we are up against a life challenge without someone to help us stay faithful to our promises, we are much more likely to fail, give up, or fall short.

Lone-ranger Christians—those without a group or community that is responsible for watching over them—are much more likely to compromise morally and spiritually and to become discouraged. The strength of mutual commitment helps us become sharper and better able to engage effectively in the battle of life.

Activity

1. Write down five activities that you would like to pursue. Consider areas of interest such as exercise, Scripture memory, cooking, hospitality, writing, learning a foreign language, leading a Bible study, etc. Consider with your friends how you might tackle one of these activities together.

2. Plan the activity. When will it happen, how often, and what will take place? Here are a few ideas to get you started:

   – Walking two and a half miles, five days a week, at 6:30 each morning
   – Forming a dinner club—gathering once a month to cook a meal together with new recipes, the fourth Monday at 6:30 p.m.
   – Meeting every Tuesday morning at Starbucks for coffee and then praying together before leaving

There are endless possibilities for how to become accountable to friends. Whatever you decide about logistics, the commitment of accountability brings a sense of belonging, a feeling of accomplishment, and a deepening of friendship.

Make a plan and begin enjoying!

PART 4
Strength

10

A Friend Inspires You to Live a Righteous Life

*The way of the righteous is like the first gleam
of dawn, which shines ever brighter until
the full light of day.*

PROVERBS 4:18

*This life therefore is not righteousness, but growth
in righteousness, not health, but healing, not being
but becoming, not rest but exercise. We are not yet
what we shall be, but we are growing toward it,
the process is not yet finished, but it is going on, this
is not the end, but it is the road. All does not yet
gleam in glory, but all is being purified.*

MARTIN LUTHER

JOY ✍ Why are the good characters always boring? This is a question that has often troubled me. Modern books and TV shows are often plagued by the stories of "good" characters who are jaw-cracking-yawn-worthily boring. I would sometimes feel bad when I felt drawn to the complex (or even bad) characters in a book or movie—not because of their badness, but because they were more interesting. I, along with Anne of Green Gables, prefer characters who could have been wicked but weren't.

I think the trouble with boring good characters has more to do with our flawed view of goodness than with goodness itself. We often think of good, moral character in terms of the negative: people who do not steal, lie, or cheat. This makes for boring characters: they are not "good" for any positive reason but because they don't do bad things. But this isn't goodness; this is simply "not badness."

This is why I like the word *righteousness*. It contains the idea that living a good or moral life is about more than just not doing bad things but about doing good things. Righteousness is about living a life marked by love, generosity, and the pursuit and proclamation of truth. With this definition, living a righteous life simply means living into our full potential as people in the image of God. We serve and love a God who is not just not bad, but who is powerful, forgiving, generous, and just—a God who is truth Himself. As we grow in knowing and loving Him, we should reflect that in our own character.

True friends want us to grow in every area of our lives. If a good friendship calls us to our best selves, it must accordingly call us to our most righteous selves. This doesn't mean that we should be constantly nitpicking our friends' moral choices but rather that we should be calling our friends to their best, most virtuous, most just, most righteous selves. A friend who does not care about our integrity or character cannot be a true friend.

Sometimes there is uneasiness around encouraging our friends to live righteous lives. What if we disagree about what a righteous life is? What if our friend thinks we are being bossy, judgmental, or legalistic? The best solution is to be humble and take the log out of our own eye, to first and always be concerned about our own integrity (Matthew 7:5). From this place of humility, we can ask our friends to hold us accountable. We can think of one another as fellow soldiers in the fight for righteousness.

Though it's not a popular idea in our culture, we need to be willing to confront and be confronted. I have been saved from so much heartache in my life because someone was willing to graciously and strongly stand up to me. Paradoxically, when a friend has confronted me, it has often made me feel loved. After all, someone who truly cares about you will not let you fail morally. A friendship that cannot survive loving conflict is not worthy of the title.

We live in a world that has long embraced the creed of "I'm okay, you're okay." But as our society has been rattled again and again by the moral failings and untempered whims of powerful people, what was always true has become powerfully evident: the choices, integrity, and righteousness of people matter.

So challenge your friends to grow into people who are not only "not bad"—but who are actively righteous, seeking justice, and fighting for integrity. The good characters don't have to be boring. In fact, in our world, I think they are the most interesting.

Activities

1. Proverbs 27:5-6 says, "Better is open rebuke than hidden love. Wounds from a friend can be trusted, but an enemy multiplies kisses" (NIV). What do you think this verse means? Since we (rightly!) want to avoid hurting or offending our friends, we generally speak about wounds as bad things. So what do you think it means for the "wounds from a friend" to be good? Have you ever been thankful that a friend confronted you? Did you accept or reject their advice? Imagine that you were about to do something morally compromising. How would you want a friend to respond to you?

2. Righteousness is not just about avoiding evil but also about pursuing good. The ancient Greeks called this idea virtue—perfecting the strength of moral character. In the third and fourth centuries, Christians adopted this idea of moral character, adding a few virtues of their own based on Scripture. They captured these virtues in the following categories:

   - *Faith:* trusting and believing in the right things
   - *Hope:* resisting cynicism; living with eternity in mind; never giving up on the possibility of redemption

74

— *Love:* caring for the good of others (physically, spiritually, and emotionally)

— *Fortitude:* brave endurance; a willingness to stick to the course even when it's difficult

— *Prudence:* the ability to determine the best course of action by looking ahead; wisdom, insight, restraint

— *Justice:* fairness in your dealings with others

— *Temperance:* being balanced; enjoying things without becoming addicted; seeking justice without becoming vengeful

All these virtues were thought to feed into each other, and as they all grow together, we become more whole and righteous. Each one of us has strengths and weaknesses in our moral character. For instance, I have a high value for justice but am not always temperate, meaning my temper can get the better of me. To grow as a person, I must learn prudence and temperance so I can pursue justice reasonably and in the right way.

Look over this list of virtues with your friends. Which do you feel strong in? Which do you feel weak in? How can you grow in these areas?

11

A Friend Supports You in Being a Good Steward of Your Body

Whether you eat or drink, or whatever you do,
do it all for the glory of God.

I CORINTHIANS 10:31

You can discover more about a person in an hour
of play than in a year of conversation.

RICHARD LINGARD, PARAPHRASED

SALLY ℘ "You look absolutely spent to your toes! Are you okay?" queried a friend. I was wrapping up a speaking engagement.

"I am not quite sure if I am okay." I had a headache, the kind I get after speaking and meeting with the people in the audience at conferences. I had just finished dealing with big teenage issues with two different teenagers for an hour apiece on the phone. Then Joy wanted to talk. And I hadn't slept well for three nights. "You are so right. I am spent all the way to my toes and trying hard not to give in to depression."

It was one of those seasons when I was feeling despair as a result of being drained on a regular basis. I had just finished speaking at the last of four weekend conferences in the span of five weeks. I know I have spent myself too much when I want to quit all my commitments and turn into a hermit.

My daughter Sarah had accompanied me to this conference, and when I got back to the hotel room, she took one look and said, "I am drawing you a warm bath and then putting you to bed."

As I soaked in the warm, sudsy water with a squeeze of citrus oil, comfort began to wash over my weariness, as soothing as a baby blanket. I barely made it into my bed, sheets rolled back, before I fell so soundly asleep I barely even remembered later how I got there.

Over coffee the next morning, as I slowly began to come to consciousness, Sarah said, "Mama, I have your next three days planned. I will be your tour guide in Asheville, and you don't have to think about anything. We will call it Sarahpy—therapy provided by Sarah for the dying of soul."

After that first Sarahpy session, Sarah and I escaped to Asheville,

North Carolina, every year for about five years in a row, following our annual series of four to six national women's conferences. The last conference was always in Raleigh, and Asheville was just a few hours away. The boys flew home to regroup, while Joy was with one of my friends for "camp time." What a reward I had awaiting me as I ended those exhausting seasons.

That first year Sarah scheduled our meals at tiny cafés with original recipes and quaint environments, including one afternoon teatime in a cozy room with windows overlooking the river-banked countryside. We shared lavender french fries with a steak at a local French café and walked miles of wild, rustic trails in sunshiny but crisp weather. I spent lots of time sleeping, sipped tea while still in bed, and paged through lovely magazines. We lit candles in our room, turned on our favorite music, and spent time in quiet, each reading a book. The coup de grâce was a hand-and-finger rub with luxurious-smelling lotion.

By the time we paid our bill and began the two-and-a-half-hour drive back to the airport, I felt like a new person. The teenagers were still having issues, and I would have bags of laundry to catch up on, mail to sort, meals to cook, and deadlines to meet when I got home. Yet having a refreshed and rested body meant that I could handle it all without falling apart.

Our bodies often take the brunt of having a too-busy life. Somehow fitting in time to take care of our physical needs seems flagrantly wasteful when there are so many duties to be attended to. But our bodies are the home, the framework, for our hearts, minds, and souls. We cannot separate our overall health from our physical needs.

It just so happens that I have lost two friends in the past few months to cancer. And I know of three friends who have been diagnosed with cancer in the last month. There are certainly many factors involved, but stress plays a role in creating a physical environment in which cancer, heart disease, diabetes, and other diseases can slowly take over our physical health.

It is easy to make our physical well-being an idol and become obsessed with our ideals about diet or exercise. That extreme is also unhealthy for our overall well-being. But speaking about physical health and habits with a friend can be a way of caring for and providing accountability for each other.

Life can be so stressful, especially when we aren't expecting it to be! So learning to manage stress is profoundly important. We need a plan to manage the stresses we face so we can flourish, the way God intended us to.

Time for a confession: I am a "stuffer." I tend to take stress into my body and do not always express what I am feeling to others. I have one relative who can give me a stomachache within a few minutes of our being together. I have learned that my best method for releasing adrenaline and stress is to walk or exercise every day, which helps me to gain control of some of the daily stress that mounts up for any number of reasons.

The following activities are designed to help you "unstuff" the stress you may be facing and learn positive coping strategies for your overall health.

Activities

1. First, take some time to evaluate the following areas of stress on your own. Make a sustainable plan within the limitations of your schedule to help you move in the direction of a healthier lifestyle—one that takes into consideration your physical needs.

Obviously, I am not a trained health care specialist; I am just offering some ideas for you to consider as you move in the direction of physical strength and well-being. The following questions are designed to give you a general overview of what kinds of health habits you have developed (and can aspire to develop).

Fun and Recreation

Sometimes the healthiest thing we can do is put aside our duties and stresses for a while and do something fun or relaxing. For example:

- a one-woman tea or coffee time for fifteen minutes so you can just sit and ponder by yourself (Stopping to rest lowers your blood pressure and your heart rate and gives your body a chance to recover.)
- a walk in nature several times a week (I recommend making this at the same time each day so it becomes built into your schedule.)
- time exercising at the gym
- a Pilates routine
- a massage, foot rub, or manicure (Physical touch not only heals the body but also brings happy hormones to our minds.)
- a fifteen-minute block of time every day to read (This takes your mind off the worry trail.)
- putting on your favorite soothing music
- tennis, running, or hiking
- gardening
- a regular game night with friends (Playing creates happy hormones that improve your physical health.)

– prayer and meditation (Time spent in prayer actually lowers your heart rate and stress levels.)

– other ideas of your own

- Name three things that you could do regularly that bring you pleasure and build your body or give you peace.

Eating and Drinking Habits

Sometimes we assume that God only cares about our souls, and what we do with our bodies does not matter, spiritually speaking. But God says that our bodies are important to Him too: "Don't you realize that your body is the temple of the Holy Spirit, who lives in you and was given to you by God?" (1 Corinthians 6:19). If our bodies are temples, that means that God cares about what we put into them.

– How many glasses of water do you drink each day?

– How many soft drinks do you consume each day?

– How many cups of caffeine do you drink daily?

– How much sugar do you put in your coffee or tea every day?

– How much alcohol do you drink each week?

– How many servings of sweets or candy do you eat every day or every week? (E.g., cake, pie, ice cream, cookies—be as specific as you want to be.)

- How many servings of fruits and vegetables do you eat daily?

- How many fast food or prepackaged meals do you eat each week?

- Do you make organic or natural foods a priority? How can you incorporate more of these foods into your daily plan?

- List three ways you plan to change to become healthier in your eating and drinking habits.

Sleeping and Resting

Our bodies need rest in order for us to accomplish the work God has called us to do and to be present for the people in our lives.

- Approximately how many hours of sleep do you get each night? What time do you go to bed?

- Do you ever take naps?

- Do you make time for a Sabbath, in which you leave the daily burdens and duties of life behind? What would a Sabbath rest look like for you (giving yourself a day off of social media, taking a long nap, walking on a nature trail, taking a Sunday afternoon drive, etc.)?

- List three ways you plan to change to become healthier in your sleeping and resting habits.

Stress

According to some estimates, about 40 million Americans suffer from some form of anxiety.[1] Regardless of our unique circumstances, we all know what it is like to deal with stress on a regular basis, whether as a result of work, ministry, family, or other relationships.

- List the activities that cause you the most stress every day or week (e.g., phone calls, social media, big messes, spending too much time in the car, etc.). Can you eliminate any of these or minimize them?

---

[1] Jamie Ducharme, "A Lot of Americans Are More Anxious Than They Were Last Year, a New Poll Says," *Time*, May 8, 2018, http://time.com/5269371/americans-anxiety-poll/.

- Name at least five ways you can simplify your life or add habits that will strengthen you physically.

2. After you have spent some time thinking about these lists on your own, talk over your answers with your friends. Share ideas for how you can encourage one another to become physically healthier and stronger. Give each person time to talk about the issues that create the most stress for her (certain relationships, financial difficulties, job-related pressures, health issues, etc.). Then pray for one another and encourage one another in these areas.

   When we allow someone else to help bear our burdens, we have the chance to cast off the heaviness of life and enter into peace.

12

A Friend Calls You to Influence Others

Let's not get tired of doing what is good.
At just the right time we will reap a harvest
of blessing if we don't give up.

GALATIANS 6:9

At times our own light goes out and is rekindled
by a spark from another person. Each of us has
cause to think with deep gratitude of those who
have lighted the flame within us.

ALBERT SCHWEITZER

SALLY ✐ Running down the cobbled street, I glanced at the aged gray stucco buildings that loomed above me on either side under the menacing January clouds. I was seeking the address of a tiny café where I had agreed to meet a friend. Finding the right name above the door, I entered a charming Austrian room, with walls covered in gold-plated mirrors. I spotted my friend and took a seat in a quaint pink-velvet-cushioned chair—also very Viennese.

I had met this young Austrian woman in the home of a friend where she was a nanny. My German was limited, as was her English, but we chatted each time I saw her. At Christmastime another friend was hosting a festive outreach for women where the Nativity story would be shared at the end of the evening. The intent was to provide an opportunity for all of us who brought friends to share Christ with them, so I had invited my new young friend to join me. The message had been in German, and as the speaker shared, I had prayed that my friend would be drawn to the personal love of God in her life.

Over the holidays, she had returned to her family in the Austrian Alps. As soon as she returned, she messaged me and asked if I would meet with her at the café.

After greeting me and sharing small tidbits about the holidays, she looked at me intently. "Sally, I was so touched by hearing that God came to earth to show us His love. I have always wanted to know that someone loved me. So over the holidays, I did what I thought was the right thing. I started reading my Bible. Do you think that is a good idea? I want to know how to know God more."

I was taken aback by her statement. She was sincerely and innocently asking me if reading the Bible was a good idea. Didn't everyone know that? But she had never been taught or heard about God's love. She was so hungry for more that I sensed she would do anything I told her to know God better. Up to that point, I had barely shared anything with her. I had spoken in my limited German and taken her to one party. Yet that was enough to touch her heart. She had been hoping and praying someone would reach out to her. I was the bumbling, fumbling woman God had used—in spite of my limitations.

As believers in Christ, we have experienced so much from the generosity of His love, goodness, and faithfulness. So the best thing we can do in friendships is to pass on the wonderful blessings we have received in growing closer to God. The best friendships are the ones in which a friend cares enough to pass on the very best of life—and for those of us who believe, that means knowing and walking with Christ every day.

In all our friendships, then, we should seek to honor Christ, encourage one another in Him, and pass on our knowledge of Him.

This is perhaps the most important chapter on friendship (which is why it's a little longer!). For Christ followers, the ultimate purpose of friendship is to spur one another on in our faith and to share the love of Christ. The deepest and most satisfying friendships come when we share the spiritual reality of walking with Christ through life. Those who know and love Christ are actually part of our spiritual family. So spiritual friendships are essential to understanding the love of God, the comfort of God, the encouragement of God, and the inspiration of God. We are given the opportunity to experience these aspects of God's character through a real, in-the-flesh person.

I was surprised by this sweet woman's response in the café, but I shouldn't have been. After all, the same thing had happened to me. As a freshman in college, I had felt lost and confused about my life. I sat on the bed in my tenth-story dorm room and prayed, sincerely, "God, if You really are there and if You care for me, would You send someone my way to tell me about You?"

And so it was, a couple of months later, that God brought a shy young woman to my door—literally. Long story short, she came into my room and shared a small booklet called *Four Spiritual Laws*. When we finished going through the little book, she asked me if I wanted to pray to have a relationship with God. She said, "Now don't feel like you have to do this right now. I can come back later."

Yet I was chomping at the bit inside. To me, she was an angel sent directly from God as an answer to my prayers. That simple moment was when I began to understand what it means to know and love God and serve Him.

Within a couple of weeks, another friend began meeting with me to do Bible study and to help me understand more of what it means to believe in Christ. I was so hungry for truth, purpose, and meaning in life that I ate up every moment we spent together.

I innocently asked a few friends on my floor if they wanted to learn some of what I was learning. And so began my first little group, who all eventually became best friends. This combination of meeting on a regular basis, eating meals out together, studying and pondering great thoughts together, and praying for one another was probably the best recipe for forming a friendship group.

Now, for the past forty-five years, I have been meeting with or organizing all sorts of small groups where women gather and seek to influence and love one another well. And because I have found love, forgiveness, grace, instruction, truth, comfort, and help from knowing and walking with God, this has become the grid through which I work in relating to others. Through them, I have found friendship, support, fun, purpose, grounding, and so much more.

Groups can take different shapes. Book clubs, meal groups, monthly gatherings, conferences, retreats, focused Bible studies, leadership groups, mother-daughter groups, church groups—all of these have filled my life over the years with sweet friendship that carries me wherever I go.

The women who express love to me and encourage me the most—the inner-circle friends who are dearest to me—all came into my life as a result of serving together in ministry. When we seek the heart of God, we find that He loves everyone we will ever meet. God would have us share His message, His touch, and His truth to those He brings into our lives. When we have this as a goal or purpose surrounding our friendships with others, we will get to watch the Holy Spirit use us and our friends to bring light to our world and to watch the transformation of people who respond to our message. This is the point of friendship—to pass on the treasures we have experienced ourselves.

When I meet a friend or enter a group, I usually ponder, *How can I add to this friend's life today? What words of encouragement might I say? How can I sympathize with her struggles right now? What thoughtful deed can I do to bring her cheer (make a meal, send flowers, write a card, ask her over for tea and chocolate)?*

Jesus chose to bring His love and redemption to the whole world through the means of relationship. Mentoring (or discipleship) is one of the ways we can build deep connection with other women. I think women are so very wonderful at bringing beauty, civilization, interest, fun, and creativity to the arenas where they invest their lives. Have I said it before? I love women.

Activities

1. Read through the following passages and answer the questions
   for yourself first. Then spend time with your friends and
   discuss your answers. Your goal at the end of this activity is to
   plan how you can reach out to friends and family with a heart
   of ministry—to make Christ real to them through what you
   say, how you serve, and what messages you live and teach. As
   you go through the verses, ask God how He wants to use your
   friendship as a means to mentor or teach others.

   Take stock of the relationships in your life. Are you in a season where you have strong friendships, good support systems,
   and a ministry community to fill your emotional and spiritual
   needs, or are you in a more isolated and lonely season? Read the
   following verses and write down how they apply to you.

   Read Ecclesiastes 4:9-12.
   - Do you have a friend who supports and stands by you—
     one you could call at any moment? Are there people who
     feel like they can call you?

   - Who is there to pick you up when you need someone to
     help you?

   - Who fights alongside you when you are attacked?

- Do you have a group that can bond together—"a cord of three strands" (verse 12, NIV)—to help all of you remain steadfast in your ideals?

Read Matthew 28:18-20.

These were the last words of Jesus recorded in Matthew. Last words usually carry extra weight, so we can assume that this final message has special significance to Jesus.

- Have you taken seriously the process of making disciples and teaching others the truth and commandments of God?

- Who are the people in your life Jesus would have you reach out to?

Read 2 Timothy 2:2.

Paul seemed to have the same message on his heart that Jesus did, instructing Timothy to find faithful people and teach them the truths Timothy had heard Paul teach so they could teach others also. Paul's ministry wasn't just about teaching the right words; it was about loving others and showing them the reality of Christ so that His good message of life and hope could spread to all people in all places in all times, so that others could also know Him.

- Who in your life is eager and enthusiastic about growing in their walk with God? Could you ask this person to lead a group with you, and then together find others to join you to grow in your walk with God?

Read Titus 2:3-4.
This final passage speaks of how God calls us to relate to one another, only this time it specifically refers to relationships between women. It's important for us to understand that it is a biblical admonition for women to encourage one another. The first part of this passage speaks of modeling a life of integrity.

- In what ways are older (or wiser, or more experienced) women supposed to be a model for younger women?

- How are older women to train younger women so they don't feel overwhelmed or alone but instead encouraged?

All four of these passages speak of passing on truth, wisdom, and discipleship. The truest friendships are built around what is true. Friendship is not just about filling our time with entertainment; it is about seeking to fulfill our deep longings for purpose, love, forgiveness, affirmation, and vision in the context of a relationship with God. Mentoring, discipleship, encouragement, and inspiration are the lens through which we need to view friendship in order to offer the best we can, which is a life of faith and faithfulness.

2. If you do not currently have a group of women or girls to meet with on a regular basis, write down the kind of group you think would help meet some of the needs in your life. There are endless possibilities for kinds of groups. Whatever our specific interests, we all need communities of women we can develop friendships with. What kind of group would you be capable of starting or leading? Here are a few examples:

  – a moms' group
  – a student group or singles' group
  – regular times with close friends
  – an interest group such as a book club, a Bible study, or an arts group

- What kind of group do you think you need? You might become the solution to your own needs! I have had to start almost every Bible study I have attended. Because we moved eighteen times after I got married, I had to learn to take initiative in order to find fellowship with like-minded people.

- Do you have a message that is on your heart? Do you have any training or experience that would qualify you to be a leader or coleader in a group?

- What messages are dear to you that God will hold you accountable for when you see Him face-to-face? What needs of others do you perceive that He might use you to meet?

- Discuss with your friend a plan for how you might be more intentional about growing in maturity and in Christ together.

- Plan a group you could colead together. Decide whom you will invite, on what day or days you will meet, and at what time. Plan the program or book you will study. Plan some light refreshments, and then step out in faith to execute your plan. You never know what friends are waiting to be found.

I have often observed that when I create space and cultivate a beautiful, welcoming environment for other women, God seems to show up, and He makes it a place of infinite blessing. (A resource you might benefit from is a small-group guide my husband, Clay, and I wrote called *Taking Motherhood to Hearts*. This book was initially written for women in our ministry to use, and it is filled with principles of how to start small groups and how to cultivate a community of like-minded women. Though some of it focuses on the role of motherhood, most of the book is a great primer for how to start a small-group ministry for any group of women.)

It is our hope and prayer that going through these activities with a friend or a group of friends has ignited new friendships that will bless and carry you with grace through the rest of your life. May the love of Christ become the foundation of your friendships, and may the grace of Christ follow you each step of your journey together.

DISCOVER THE GIFT OF FRIENDSHIP!